"Where should Product Managers invest their time to improve their productivity, effectiveness, and career growth? 'The Phenomenal Product Manager' answers this question by presenting proven tips and techniques for anyone who must lead without authority or finds themselves in 'reaction mode' far more than desired."
Michael J. Salerno, Co-founder, Boston Product Management Association

"This is a book on how Product Managers can successfully conduct themselves with teams, customers and most importantly upper management. I absolutely recommend this book for anyone new to Product Management or seeking tips on being more effective with the people in their organizations."
Therese Padilla, Co-Founder, AIPMM (Association for International Product Marketing & Management)

"The Phenomenal Product Manager is a must-read for every Product Manager who wants to be more successful. Full of tips and strategies from a 25 year career in Product Management, it covers the real-world part of Product Management that no other book out there addresses."
Mike Freier, President, Silicon Valley Product Management Association

"There are those that teach and those that do—Brian Lawley is one of the few that knows how to do both."
John Cook, Vice President, WW Desktop Marketing Hewlett-Packard Corporation

"As a Product Manager, you can write great requirements and market analyses but unless you garner support from all the various stakeholders your work will at best be academic. 'The Phenomenal Product Manager' helps you be more than just a sufficient Product Manager, but an irreplaceable one."
Alyssa Dver, CPM, CPPM, Author, 'Software Product Management Essentials' & 'No Time Marketing'

The Phenomenal Product Manager

By Brian Lawley

20660 Stevens Creek Blvd., Suite 210
Cupertino, CA 95014

Dedication

This book is dedicated to all of those brave souls who choose Product Management as a profession because they want to bring products into the world that truly make a difference.

It is also dedicated to my family, the 280 Group team and my late wife Sarah (without her this book, the 280 Group and our daughter Taylor would never have been possible).

A Message from Happy About®

Thank you for your purchase of this Happy About book. It is available online at http://happyabout.info/phenomenal-product-manager.php or at other online and physical bookstores.

- Please contact us for quantity discounts at sales@happyabout.info
- If you want to be informed by email of upcoming Happy About® books, please email bookupdate@happyabout.info

Happy About is interested in you if you are an author who would like to submit a non-fiction book proposal or a corporation that would like to have a book written for you. Please contact us by email editorial@happyabout.info or phone (1-408-257-3000).

Other Happy About books available include:

- Expert Product Management:
  http://happyabout.info/expertproductmanagement.php
- Expert Product Management Toolkit Bundle:
  http://happyabout.info/expertproductmanagement.php
- Scrappy Project Managment:
  http://happyabout.info/scrappyabout/project-management.php
- 42 Rules™ for Creating WE:
  http://happyabout.info/42rules/creatingwe.php
- 42 Rules™ of Employee Engagement:
  http://happyabout.info/42rules/employee-engagement.php
- 42 Rules for Successful Collaboration:
  http://www.happyabout.info/42rules/successful-collaboration.php
- 42 Rules™ to Jumpstart Your Professional Success:
  http://happyabout.info/42rules/jumpstartprofessionalservices.php
- I'm on LinkedIn -- Now What???:
  http://happyabout.info/linkedinhelp.php
- Twitter Means Business:
  http://happyabout.info/twitter/tweet2success.php
- Blitz the Ladder:
  http://happyabout.info/blitz.php
- Internet Your Way to a New Job:
  http://happyabout.info/InternetYourWaytoaNewJob.php
- The Successful Introvert:
  http://happyabout.info/thesuccessfulintrovert.php
- Happy About an Extra Hour Every Day:
  http://happyabout.info/an-extra-hour.php

Contents

Contents

Introduction

There are many books, white papers and reference materials that teach Product Management and product marketing techniques and best practices. If you want to learn to write excellent market requirements, build a business case, position a product or do a full-scale launch you can learn how to do so in a variety of ways.

However, learning these skills is not nearly enough. During my 25-year career in Product Management and product marketing I have seen hundreds of smart, capable people who had the skills described above yet either failed or were mediocre at what they did. Many of these people could not understand why they couldn't rise up to the next level and be highly effective.

This book is about learning the other fifty percent that makes a Product Manager or Product Marketer incredibly successful. It is based on my observations of excellence in others as well as strategies and tactics I have personally used to succeed. It is also about getting more enjoyment out of the profession of Product Management and about how to move your career forward in a systematic and planned way.

My hope is that this book will help the hundreds of thousands of Product Managers and Product Marketers throughout the world to be more successful in their careers, more satisfied in their jobs and to create products that truly delight their customers and are highly profitable to their companies.

phe·nom·enal (adjective)

- extraordinary; highly remarkable

pro·duct man-a-ger (noun)

- Someone with all of the responsibility and little or no authority

- A person who loves bringing great products to life

- The one person who has the ability to dramatically affect a product's success or failure

1 Product Marketing versus Product Management

Before we begin we need to clarify the terms we are using and the roles and responsibilities that we will be talking about.

From here on out we will be using the term Product Manager to refer to both Product Managers and Product Marketers. The titles are used in a variety of ways and definitions vary greatly across different companies. All of the skills in this book can be applied to both positions, but it is important to understand how we view them, as some skills will be more important depending on how the roles are defined.

The easiest way to think about the difference between these two is to think of them as **inbound** and **outbound**. Inbound (Product Management) spends most of their time with engineering teams and customers, making critical decisions and ensuring that everything gets done to bring customer-focused products to market. Outbound (Product Marketing) makes sure that once these products are ready, they get launched and marketed effectively to the target customer base.

Here's a summary of the typical duties under each role:

Product Management

- Market Analysis, Business Cases and Profit and Loss Investigation

- Customer and Market Research

- Writing Marketing Requirements Documents (MRDs)

- Working with Engineering to finalize functional specifications

- Competitive analysis for use internally at the company

- Analysis of technology trends

- Running alpha/beta programs and capturing early customer feedback

- Making feature, schedule and cost tradeoffs as the product nears completion

Product Marketing

- Writing product launch plans

- Product Messaging, including Positioning, Features and Benefits and Unique Selling Proposition (USP)

- Developing sales tools: white papers, presentations, collateral, competitive analyses for external use with customers

- Working with PR to manage launch tours and product review programs

- Setting product pricing

- Working with beta sites to generate customer success stories

- Running product launches

- Working with sales, channel marketing, corporate marketing, marketing communications, technical support, finance, operations and other departments to ensure the product is effectively intro-duced to the market and continues to be successful

Some companies make a clear distinction of the roles and responsibilities in each of these areas, and have dedicated employees for each. They may have dedicated Product Managers, whose entire role is to work with engineers to make sure that the products being built meet customer needs and requirements. They may also have dedicated Product Marketing Managers who become involved as the product nears completion, managing the launch, messaging, training of the sales force, and ongoing support to ensure continued success (briefing customers and the channel, working with press and analysts, etc.).

In other companies one individual wears both hats and performs all of the tasks above. That person may be called a Product Manager or a Product Marketing Manager. Many times the title given has little to do with what they are actually doing. It may be politically incorrect to have the word "Marketing" in their title, particularly if they report into engineering or another functional area. Or, the word Marketing may be left out if their engineering team has a strong bias against working with "Marketing people."

One item to note: it's a rare breed of person who can effectively manage and enjoy doing all aspects of both these positions. When you are choosing what role you want for your job, make sure that you pick one that fits your strengths.

There are many people who are incredibly good at, and happy doing, Product Management who would fail miserably at Product Marketing, and vice versa. If this is the case for you then doing what you are good at will lead you to much success. If you do decide to take a job that has a hybrid model (where one person owns everything) make sure that you get the training you need to beef up your areas of weakness.

If you are particularly strong at one area and do not have an interest or aptitude for the other, don't worry. I have known many people who went the Product Management or the Product Marketing route and have done great in their careers. Just make sure that you are suited for and interested in the role you agree to take on—otherwise you may find yourself delivering sub-optimal performance and having a miserable time.

Chapter 1: Product Marketing versus Product Management

2 What is a Phenomenal Product Manager?

If you have been in Product Management for a while, you probably have come across a few Product Managers who seem to stand out. For some reason they come across as being really good at what they do, whereas other Product Managers seem to have little or no clue. They are the stars—the phenomenal Product Managers who are clearly on the road to big things in their careers.

Thinking about the Product Managers that I have known over my career there are a number of characteristics that they seem to have in common:

- **Vision:** The ability to see where the market, competition and industry are going and to create a strong vision for where their product needs to be in order to win the market and satisfy customers. This includes both short-term and long-term thinking, and often-times requires defying what others in the company may believe because they do not have as much information or customer and market insight as the Product Manager does.

- **Boldness:** If you have great ideas but don't have the guts to stand up and fight for them you will never succeed as a Product Manager. You are much better off taking a job where you can voice safe opinions. There was a time early in my career where I was somewhat afraid to be bold and it was not pleasant.

- **Ability to Influence:** The ability to use both logic and emotion to win over wide ranges of audiences to your point of view as you are implementing the product vision and strategy that you believe in.

- **Leadership:** Being able to lead your extended team without any formal authority. Building enough credibility and respect so that others are motivated to let you be in charge of a product line's future.

- **Expertise:** Being an expert in both the field of Product Management as well as the market segments your product is targeted to. If you aren't an expert about the customers, markets, technology and trends for your product then it is difficult to get others to follow you.

- **Enthusiasm:** Enthusiasm is contagious. If you have a strategy and vision and are enthusiastic, you can bring others along with you in your efforts.

NOTE: The opposite is even more true.

If you are jaded and negative you will ultimately fail with both your product and your career advancement. This is a trap that I see far too many Product Managers fall into—they think that being jaded and cynical is humorous and don't realize the damage they are doing to themselves and their product.

- **Tenacity:** The ability to keep going despite facing difficult people and circumstances.

- **Commitment to Excellence:** This includes excellence in both the work you do and deliverables (presentations, market requirements, business cases, etc.) as well as the details of the product itself. The Product Manager is at the center of all aspects of the product. If they don't own delivering excellence for all aspects of the product, no one else will.

This might seem like an overwhelming set of qualities to develop and focus on, but don't worry. The more you practice them the easier it becomes. Just becoming aware of them gives you a big advantage over other Product Managers. Additionally, many of these are the qualities that you need in order to advance your career no matter what you want to do, whether you stay in Product Management, become a senior executive or move on to being a CEO.

Worksheet: Becoming a Phenomenal Product Manager

Rank yourself from 1 to 5 for each characteristic, where 1 indicates greatest strength and 5 indicates greatest need to develop in this area:

Vision
1   2   3   4   5

Boldness
1   2   3   4   5

Ability to Influence
1   2   3   4   5

Leadership
1   2   3   4   5

Expertise
1   2   3   4   5

Enthusiasm
1   2   3   4   5

Tenacity
1   2   3   4   5

Commitment to Excellence
1   2   3   4   5

List three specific things you are going to do to improve in these areas.

1. _____

2. _____

3. _____

3 Influencing Engineers

Now we are going to discuss how to work more effectively with your engineering team and individual engineers. In my opinion, your ability to influence and work effectively with engineers is a huge part of whether or not you'll be successful as a Product Manager, and also whether you'll be satisfied with your job. If you can't get your engineers to build the product that you believe meets customer needs and moves forward on your vision, then your product will fail and so will you.

The question I would ask you to think about right now is, "Are you succeeding or failing in terms of working with your engineers?" Are you able to influence them? Are you able to get on the same page with them and build a sense of a team? Or are you simply viewed as somebody who has the word "marketing" in their title and as a result, not somebody whom engineers can take seriously.

I've worked with some excellent teams over my career, and some that were not so excellent (and several that just plain sucked). I would imagine everybody out there has had similar experiences. I worked with engineering teams at Apple and

Symantec, at start-ups and as a consultant for the past 10 years, so I've seen a broad range of engineers and teams.

One team that I worked with at Apple literally refused to let any Product Manager attend their team meetings. Basically, they'd ask Product Managers to just check in every two months to receive an update on their "progress." They were building a product with no customer input, had spent several man-years of engineering effort and didn't have a clear definition of what the final shipping product would do or how it would benefit customers. And they had no intention of bringing in a Product Manager to help them figure it out (mainly because my predecessor had been incredibly incompetent). Incidentally, after a few months of focusing on the other products I was working on I let them know that unless we changed the approach we would not be shipping the product to customers. Realizing they needed my assistance (at least to launch the product) we began to work together again as a team.

If you end up with a team like that, obviously it has its own challenges. But don't be surprised if you end up in this situation. Product Management is so misunderstood that teams will likely have some negative preconceived notions. The good news is that when you come in as a competent Product Manager and play your part many teams will be enthused to have your help.

In this chapter we'll talk about how to adjust your strategies based on personalities and based on your team and how cooperative or uncooperative they are. There are six techniques that we will be discussing. I would encourage you to think about what are you doing actively right now in all six areas to improve your effectiveness.

Credibility

We'll start by talking about credibility. As a Product Manager oftentimes you go into situations with engineers where the deck is stacked against you. They may have worked with somebody who was not a particularly good Product Manager, someone who was dishonest with them or had broken their trust. Or they may simply have no idea what the role of a real Product Manager is and may not understand why they need someone in that role.

Your challenge is going to be to build credibility around all of this. You need to show them what you are doing, why you are doing it and make sure they view you as an expert in a range of different areas.

For example, if you're not able to establish enough technical credibility with your engineering team, many times they simply won't give you any respect and they won't work with you. Your ability to influence them will be very, very trivialized. It's absolutely critical that you establish that you are a technical expert. You have to follow the trends that are going on in your area of technology. You have to know the acronyms and the terminology. It's not so much that you have to be a complete expert and understand all of the underpinnings of the technology, but what you do have to prove to your team is that you have the ability to understand.

If your team is talking about software architecture, for instance, you have to show that you have the ability to ask the right questions, really get to the fundamental understanding of the implications of the decisions and form some strong opinions about them.

This is also true if you're working with anything having to do with stan-dards. I'll give you a simple example. I had one team that was creating a product using FreeBSD, an open-source Unix operating system. The market was going towards Linux. Being able to talk about the trends and the underlying technology and its advantages and disadvantages was absolutely critical because the value of the intellectual property and the momentum of the marketplace were at stake (incidentally, I lost this argument).

You also need to establish yourself as a domain expert in the Product Management domain. It's critical that not just your engineering team but everyone in your company views you as someone who under-stands Product Management inside and out. You wouldn't want to hire a chief financial officer or an accountant to do their job if you didn't know that they knew it inside and out, and Product Management is no different.

You need to know best practices. You need to be able to say confident-ly, "This is the wrong approach. Most companies do it the following way." You also need corresponding tools for creating Business Cases, Market Requirements Documents (MRDs), Product Requirements Documents (PRDs), Use Cases etc.

Whether you are using a solution like the Product Manager's Toolkit from the 280 Group (a collection of templates covering the entire product lifecycle) or some other solution, you will have much more credibility if you are using an established methodology. If you have an efficient set of tools and best practices you can show your team and use in action it will oftentimes go a long way towards establishing credibility with your engineers. Engineering spends a huge amount of time thinking about the tools they are using and how to be more efficient and how to implement best practices, etc. If you do the same thing on the Product Management side, that will boost your credibility.

Certainly any training you can go through and any certifications you can get will increase your domain credibility. If you become a certified Product Manager through the AIPMM (Association of International Product Marketing and Management), for instance, and you hang your certification in your office cube your team will see this and understand that you truly have studied this discipline and that you are excellent at what you do.

Another critical area of credibility is market expertise. You have to know more about your market than anyone in your entire company. You need to understand growth rates and competition and you need to be able to have facts and data ready that you can bring up in discussions. Any time that you can use data about your market in discussions it will help to establish you as the market expert. There should be no one on your team who knows as much about your market as you do. You want to be viewed from the business side as completely understanding your market.

Correspondingly, you also want to be viewed as the person who is the true voice of the customer. You'll know you've achieved this when your engineering team is struggling over an issue and they come to you proactively to ask you, "We could do it this way or that way; which way do you think the customers will want it?" At that point, you've established yourself as the real expert who has a finger on the pulse of the customer.

How do you establish yourself as the voice of the customer? Make lots of customer visits. For each customer visit, write up a summary of what you found. Include stories about what happened and information about the customer environment. Continually bring up the customer in your conversations and remind engineers that you've spent significant time with them.

Another good tactic is to bring your engineers along if you possibly can. It's always extremely valuable to take engineers out in the field and have them meet some customers and observe what you do as a Product Manager in terms of the kind of questions you ask, etc.

Building Rapport with the Team

In addition to establishing technical, market and domain credibility (as well as having an ear to the voice of the customer) it's also absolutely critical to build good rapport with your team. You must build great rapport so that when it comes down to a difficult situation, if you need to ask for a favor or for the team's support, you can.

The key to building real rapport is sincerity, and there are many ways (both subtle and not) to sincerely develop rapport. Obviously grabbing lunch or coffee together is a good thing. When was the last time you bought your whole engineering team lunch and had it brought in? Or when was the last time you took some engineers out after work to get to know them? You can also give people small gifts (the latest tech gadget or something cool for their office). If you can bring donuts to your weekly team meetings, you'll find attendance will go up dramatically and you are developing a better working relationship. This sounds too simple to be true, but you would be amazed how small things add up. I actually had one team meeting where people would show up extra early because they wanted to get their favorite donut.

If you go to trade shows, pick up tchotchkes (give away items) such as USB thumb drives or other things for your team. Engineers don't get the chance to go out on the road and attend trade shows, so oftentimes if you can bring them something back that's a nice freebie it can go a long way.

In terms of gifts, learn what your team likes and keep an eye out for opportunities. One of the things I did with one of my teams (this was back when Nintendo 64 was brand new and it was very difficult to get extra controllers) was to buy extras when I happened to find them in stock at a store. The team was psyched and it helped us build rapport and trust.

One of the best ways to build rapport is to always have the coolest new gadget. Always be asking your team what their opinion is, which one you should get, etc. For example, "If I get a PS-3 is it really a good Blue Ray player or should I buy a separate one?" If you talk about games, gadgets and cool new technology many of your engineers will all of a sudden view you very differently from being just that Product Manager guy or gal.

The next concept in terms of building rapport is to not cry wolf. You've probably all seen this before (or done it yourselves). There will be a Product Manager who constantly goes back to the engineering team with frantic new requests. This is often justified by the competitive environment changing, an urgent request from sales or a large customer or a variety of other things. If you go to your team often and try to tell them the sky is falling, if you cry wolf over and over again, there will come a point where your credibility and your ability to influence people will be completely shot.

Instead you need to be very careful about how you approach things. It's not to say you can't go back and ask for changes, but you really don't want to be known as the person who is constantly trying to change priorities every other day.

Going along with that is sort of the opposite concept. Once you really build rapport and get to know your team and things are going well, you do have the ability to occasionally play a chip and ask for a change that might otherwise seem unreasonable. You can't do this constantly, but if done right and sparingly it can be very effective.

For example, there was a situation at Apple when I was a Product Manager where the printer drivers that we were working with were causing a significant delay in printing in certain circumstances. There was a vocal minority of customers (though large enough to warrant taking action) who were really pissed off about it. I knew the right engineer quite well and had built a rapport with him. I went and talked to him and told him I was really concerned about what the customers were going through. He respected my opinion enough that without me even having to ask he worked over the weekend and fixed the problem so that the printing took 3 seconds instead of three and a half minutes.

If I hadn't built up the rapport, really gotten to know the engineer and built up the trust that I was the voice of the customer, he might have not been willing to spend any time on fixing it. But I had gotten to know him well enough, and also he knew that I didn't come and ask for favors and I didn't cry wolf every other day. If I brought something up, it was truly important and I had the credibility to be able to pull it off.

Assessing Your Team and Adjusting

In working with your team it is important for you to read the team you are dealing with and then adjust accordingly. The chart below shows some of the scenarios you will encounter.

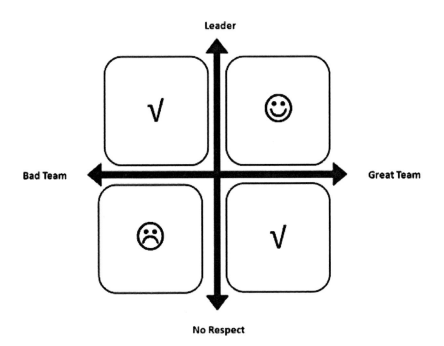

In some cases you'll have a great team where you can easily establish yourself as a leader. When you are in the upper right quadrant this is when Product Management is a really, really fun job.

On the flip side, there are some teams and situations where there's nothing you can do. You may be in that bottom left quadrant, and you may seriously need to think about whether you want to move on to a different product or move to work with a different team. There are some situations where there is simply no way to win. Don't let yourself get stuck for a long time in one of these—it is a career-limiting move.

In my career, when I had a good boss, an interesting product and a great team this was the time that I enjoyed my work the most and also was most effective. There are some bad teams I worked with where I should have cut my losses earlier and moved on.

If you are in either one of the check-marked quadrants you can definitely make it work and can move towards the upper right quadrant. In most situations that's where you'll be as a Product Manager.

In addition to the team, you must assess the personality types of the people you are working with. There are three major types of personalities that I have found in engineers.

One would be the prima donna. That's an engineer who's absolutely brilliant and who insists on having an argument about everything to make sure that they get to the truth (though usually they have already made up their mind about what the truth is). Oftentimes they'll be really excellent at what they do, but they won't necessarily know or care about the role of Product Management. Your job in working with a prima donna is to make them hungry for real-world data about customers and the market that only you can provide. And if you can present arguments such that they draw logical conclusions that they believe they have come to on their own, so much the better.

At the other extreme is what I would call a coder. A coder is somebody who doesn't have strong opinions, but rather says, "Tell me exactly what to build. Give me a spec. I just write code. I'll add any feature you want. I'll do anything you want, just be very clear and very specific." The challenge here is that you had better be very specific or you may end up with something very different from what you originally envisioned. A great approach here is to write requirements and then work very closely with the coder to iterate so that they don't get too far down the wrong path.

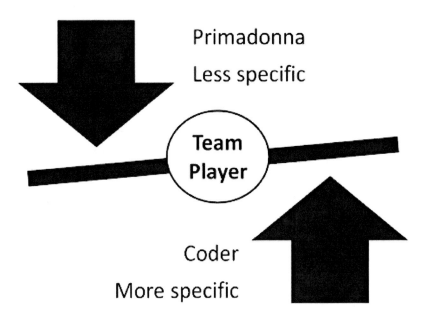

Primadonna
Less specific

Team
Player

Coder
More specific

In between the coder and the prima donna is what I would call a team player. The team player understands the value you're bringing, and they really want to work with you in an interactive fashion to build a product that customers love. If you give them requirements and allow them to creatively come up with a solution they will oftentimes blow you away with the elegance and creativity they display.

Sometimes you'll have entire teams that have these three characteristics. More often you'll have a variety of individuals that span the range. You need to adjust your strategy based on who you're talking to on the team and decide what will be most effective in influencing them to build a great product for your customers.

For a prima donna, for instance, when you are delivering a market requirements or product requirements document or specifying some features, you probably want to be a little bit less specific about exactly how they should be implemented. You might want to put a recommen-dation in that says, "Customers need to be able to do the following. Here's one way you might do it but this is just an idea." Let the prima donna solve it—in fact challenge him or her to come up with a great solution. Ask them for their opinions, and why they want to do things the way they are proposing. Is it really the best way to solve the problem? Play to their ego.

On the flip side, for a coder, be as specific as you possibly can and basically tell him or her how it should be. This is exactly what I need—the following feature needs to be implemented this way. I'm not sure how to necessarily do the UI or do this portion of the design, so you come back with a design and I'll approve it. Again, as you are going along communicate with them and reassure them that they are on track in delivering what you want.

If you take this strategy and you start to characterize the different people that you work with, you'll be far more effective. Conversely, if you try to take the approach you would use with the coder and apply it to a prima donna or vice versa you will fail miserably. Trust me, I have made that mistake for you.

Communication

This is one of the most critical areas. The first part of good communi-cation is making sure that everyone you are working with understands your role. This is because in most companies the role of Product Man-agement is misunderstood and not well defined. The executives, the engineers and the sales people don't really get what it is that a Product Manager does.

Everyone who's been a Product Manager knows that you literally must do hundreds of small things to make your product successful. But for most of those things, unless you actively communicate about what you are doing, the people around you are not going to know what you are actually working on.

I suggest you put together a quick presentation that covers your role and responsibilities and present it (either informally or formally) to your engineering team, sales team and managers. There is a white paper called Product Marketing versus Product Management on http://www.280group.com that can help you with putting together a presentation.

A second part of communication is to make sure that as your engineers are writing code and stressing to make deadlines they understand that you are working hard doing the things that need to be done for a successful launch. You need to reassure them that you are doing everything possible to make the product a success, and you want them to know that you are as committed to shipping and succeeding with this product as they are.

One way to do that is to share your status reports with them. This makes you publicly accountable and can provide visibility into the many things that a Product Manager spends time on that their team doesn't necessarily know about. When I've done this in the past I'll simply copy my engineering team when I send a status report to my boss. Oftentimes, they'll look at the list and realize just how much I am doing and what I am spending my time on. I have found they will have a lot more respect for me rather than wondering what it is I do between team meetings.

Another key concept of communication is early buy in. What you don't want to do is surprise your engineering team constantly. When you deliver a market requirements document, product requirements or a roadmap you want to have talked through the draft ideas with them and you want them to understand the process you're going through. If you're prioritizing features, you want them to understand the matrix you are using and the methodology. In general, the earlier that you get buy in the better the results will be.

Influencing

The fifth concept for working more effectively with your engineers is influencing. There are many things that you can do to influence your team, and I will share a few things that have worked for me in the past.

The first one is to always have a variety of customer stories ready to use. When you're talking about or debating whether to add a feature or how important it is, if you have some anecdotal stories that you can bring up (for example, when I was at customer A they told me such and such) it will help greatly to argue your points. Engineers may disagree with your opinion but it is hard to disagree with a customer's opinion.

Additionally, whenever you do customer visits make sure you summarize the discussions and send them out to the team. Use a standard format so that they are well organized and easy to read and archive. If at all possible bring a video camera and get some video footage, and show a few select clips. Presenting the data in a methodical way will have much more weight than if you simply write a few random emails with customer requests in them.

For example, at Apple we did some focus groups around a new release of the operating system. We had been trying to tell the engineering team that there was a major problem when you installed fonts. When you dragged fonts to the system folder the computer would completely lock up for about 30 seconds. You'd get no indication anything was happening, and customers would think that their computer had crashed.

There were many complaints about this, and we tried to influence the engineers and get them to make a change and optimize it. However, their point of view was that people don't install fonts very often so it really wasn't an important issue.

To influence the engineers in this particular case we showed some clips from the focus groups. One of the clips was a customer saying, "I can't believe how bad this is. I thought my machine had completely crashed. I rebooted it and the problem continues to happen. You have to fix this problem."

Lo and behold, between when we showed the video on Friday and the next Monday one of the engineers had cranked out a fix over the weekend. All of a sudden it was so much more important—not because Product Management said so but because they experienced the customer frustration and heard it loud and clear.

A second way of influencing is to use data everywhere you possibly can. When you write a product requirements or market requirements document, and you're talking about a specific feature, put in some data about why it's important. For example, "In our last customer survey, 73 percent of customers said that this was critical."

The more data-driven you are, the more your engineers will respect you. They may question the data but oftentimes if you put forth compelling arguments that are backed by data your ability to get what you want is dramatically enhanced.

The last technique in terms of influencing is what I call the "Three Reasons" technique. I use this all the time. The way it works is that when you are debating a point you state your point and indicate that it is correct for three reasons. For example, "We need to add feature X for three reasons." Then come up with the best three reasons that you can think of on the spot.

Why does this technique work? First, just claiming you have three reasons makes your argument appear to be strong. Second, oftentimes you won't have three reasons thought through, but saying this and talking about the first one will give you time to come up with the second and third (and in many cases you won't even have to talk about the second and third reasons). Even if the other reasons are weak it is better than a one-point argument. And third, it makes your argument sounds more official and well-thought-out so that people will buy into it. This may sound far-fetched, but you will be amazed at how well this can work for you. I'd encourage you to try to this and whenever possible come up with three reasons.

Worksheet: Working more effectively with your engineering teams

Rank yourself from 1 to 5 for each characteristic, where 1 indicates you need to improve and 5 indicates complete mastery:

Credibility
1   2   3   4   5

Rapport
1   2   3   4   5

Assessing and Adjusting
1   2   3   4   5

Communication
1   2   3   4   5

Influencing
1   2   3   4   5

List three concrete steps you are going to take to improve in each of these areas.

1. _____

2. _____

3. _____

What are you going to ask your manager or team to do to help you with improving in this area?

_____

_____

4 Leveraging Your Sales Team

A Product Manager's sales team can be their best ally or their worst nightmare. When armed properly, incented correctly and enthused about your products they can make the difference between failure and massive success. This chapter is about how to get them on your side, and will cover a number of tactics I have used successfully.

Motivation

The first tactic is to make sure you understand the motivation of a salesperson. Understanding the motivation behind sales people and how they think is critical. As Product Managers and Product Marketers oftentimes we're motivated by different things. I think part of our motivation tends to be that we want to build great products and make them successful in the market. Sales people, on the other hand, are motivated very differently.

It is quite simple—money is the key. That's why people go into sales—they have a big upside opportunity and the chance to make a lot of money. You want to make sure that it is incredibly easy for them to sell your product and make more than they expected. If you're at a company that has 50 different products, you want them to be able to sell yours so easily that it's a complete no-brainer. Do this and you will have them on your side.

WIIFM

The second tactic is that you have to be incredibly crisp and clear about what I call WIIFM or "What's in it for me?" You have to be able to tell them in less than 1 minute why they should be focusing on your product, why it's worth their while and why you're making it easy to sell. This includes how they can easily cross-sell and upsell customers with other products. It includes how they can add on consulting, support and other ongoing revenue streams. And it includes convincing them that the solution is excellent for customers so that they don't have to spend time fixing problems and instead can focus on closing new deals.

The WIIFM factor is incredibly important. I'll give you an example of this. One of our consulting clients was a company called SEMI, and they were launching a new online directory. We were dependent on their sales reps who sell advertising in their magazine to also sell space in the online directory.

What we did was that we got together with one of their top sales reps. She was initially very hesitant to sell this because it was completely different from anything she had sold before. We gave her the pitch. We told her how she could sell it—it was an easy add-on sale to the advertising her customers were already buying. We included bundle pricing to make it simple to explain and upsell. And we included a forecast of how much incremental revenue and commission she could make in the next year just by adding this into the sales conversation with her customers.

What ended up happening was that we formed an alliance with her. We set her up so she understood what was in it for her. She made a sale to the first customer she presented it to, and as a result we were able to use her as a success story with the other reps. When some of the other reps indicated they thought it might be too difficult to sell we were able to have her tell them that it was a no-brainer.

Think of your sales people as allies. Whenever I've been a Product Manager, I've tried to find three to five sales people who were in my corner. I'll do lots of favors for them. I'll buy them lunch. I'll get to know them really well. I will go out of my way to visit their customers if they ask.

I had a powerful sales ally when I was at Apple. She worked in New York City and many of the big customers for Apple at the time were the advertising agencies there. She and I became very good allies. She would call on me when she needed a favor. If she had a client who wanted an advance briefing or if she had a really important meeting with the executives at a large client, she would call me and I would do demos and fly out to meet with them. But then she also did favors for me. She would get me access to the key decision makers when I had critical things I needed to talk about in terms of product futures.

She gave me great feedback on the selling tools I provided, and would let the other reps know about them when they became available. She would back me up if I needed a voice from the field for critical product or strategy decisions. And the feedback she provided from customers was tremendously valuable.

Identify the Target

The next tactic is to make sure your sales people understand who the target is and that they're selling to the right customer. You want to paint a picture to them about how big the market is and what the opportunity is. Make sure they understand it is a large market that has great potential for them. And teach them about the buyers and the buying process so that they can be as effective as possible.

It's great if you can share personas from your market requirements and product requirements documents. Give them the persona for the user, decision maker and purchaser and tell them what the motivation is and why your product is a perfect fit. This will allow them to understand the customer pain points and the motivation for purchasing.

As a Product Manager, you have probably experienced the situation where a sales rep is out trying to sell the wrong product to a customer. If you don't educate them about who to target they will go after all kinds of different customers, so it is your job to make sure they know who to sell to.

For example, in the 1990's I worked for a company that made Internet appliances for small business. The entire company strategy was to penetrate the small business, and the product, pricing and all other aspects of the mix were designed accordingly.

Nonetheless, I had a couple of sales reps who would try to go in and get large corporate deals. They'd try to sell to branch offices of Fortune 500 companies, and spent quite a bit of time and energy doing so. Of course the problem was that the product was optimized for small business. It was not designed for branch offices or for corporate sales, and it would have taken a good 2 years to build a product for that market. I had to constantly try to re-educate them about who the target customer was so that they didn't spin their wheels trying to sell a solution that didn't fit.

The other thing about providing the target customer and market data to them is that if they come back with a customer who is outside of the target you can say no to feature requests. This gives you a way let them know that when they find the right customer you will help them to make the sale, but until then they shouldn't be requesting features that are not for the target customer.

Great Leads

The next tactic is making sure the leads you get to them are very well qualified. You know the old saying—garbage in equals garbage out. Whether you actually run the lead generation programs or whether you're a Product Manager and you hand it to product marketing or a marketing department who does lead generation, ultimately the person who owns the success of your product is you. So you have got to make sure your lead generation programs are going to get to that target customer and are really going to work. You really need to take a leadership position here in terms of working with your marketing department and making sure that the leads they send to your sales guys are well qualified.

Why is this critical? Well, if they get leads that are not well qualified they'll basically pound their head on the wall trying to close the leads or turn them into prospects and eventually they'll quit. They'll quit trying to sell your product and they'll either come back and tell you that:

1. the leads you're giving them are just garbage or
2. the product just won't sell.

Either situation will stall or kill your product's overall success.

If you want to truly be responsible for the success of your product, you have to make sure that good leads are getting in their hands. By the way, my definition of a great Product Manager is someone who owns everything about the product in terms of success—customer satisfaction, the sales process, everything—and make sure that product is going to be as successful as possible.

Messaging

The next tactic is messaging. You have to have a compelling elevator pitch (i.e. be able to explain the product in an elevator in 10 floors or less). You need to nail your product positioning. You need to have a Unique Selling Proposition (USP) that is very hard hitting. You should be able to get it across in literally 30 seconds.

If you create compelling messaging your sales reps are going to be able to repeat it's going to be believable and it's going to be credible. Ideally, the rep should be able to sit down with any customer and very quickly convey why they should be interested in purchasing the product. If you can get your messaging to that point, you'll have a much higher chance of success.

Excellent Sales Tools

The next tactic, and this is probably the most important, is to provide excellent sales tools. Your sales tools have to be simple and effective and they have to make it incredibly easy for the rep to make the sale. Done right they will provide you with tremendous leverage.

If you're a Product Manager and you're constantly being asked by sales to be involved with customer visits or to provide additional information you probably don't have good sales tools in place. If you have excellent sales tools, it allows the sales reps (or sales engineers) to tell the whole story and it basically gives them the ammunition to go out and get the sale without having to get you involved.

Make sure that your set of sales tools is complete. Include a data sheet, brochure, self-running demos, videos, demo scripts, FAQs, volume pricing calculators, white papers and a quick selling sheet (a quick selling sheet is just a one-page document with the USP for the product, with five reasons why a customer should buy it and the top five features and benefits).

Make sure you provide them with qualification questions so that they can get to whether or not this is a qualified prospect. Also give them a presentation, competitive handouts, price lists, and ROI calculators.

Here's the point. If you don't provide all of these things, you're going to be asked for them. If you don't have a really good set of competitive handouts, what will happen is your reps will come back to you and in a fire drill manner tell you they need it now or they need you to be involved in the conversation. Likewise with all of the other materials—you can either create them up-front or you can be inundated daily with requests. If you can put together a really excellent set of sales tools and run your sales reps through a quick training so that they understand the basic details it will make your life much easier.

Also make sure to provide sales tools for all of your channel partners. Your channel partners are even more removed from your company and from the commitment to making your company and your product successful. They just want to sell whatever is easiest to sell that makes the most money, so you have to set them up for success.

For example, when I was at Apple Computer and also at Claris Corporation we decided to redesign our packaging. We went out and observed the selling environment and the channel to make sure our packaging would work. One of the things we found in the channel, particularly at the retail level, was that retail reps knew very little or nothing about our products. In fact, much of the information they provided was wrong.

The way that they explain a product to a customer is that they pick up the box and read the bullet points to them. If they are talking to a customer on the phone they read the bullet points on the data sheet or in their sales system. So if you don't have great bullet points or information on your packaging and other sales materials the chances that the retail reps are going to be able to sell your products are very low.

Upsell and Ongoing Revenues

The next tactic to leverage is upsell and ongoing revenue.

One of the best ways to incent sales reps to focus on your product is look at your product lines and see what's selling the best. What are your most popular products? If you can tie your product into a sale with the popular ones and provide the sales reps with a simple way to present and sell it, it's going to make your product a lot more successful.

You also want to make sure that sales reps understand they're not just making a one time sale with your product. If there's a recurring revenue stream they make a commission from or any other possible source of ongoing revenue you want to make this as obvious as possible to them.

Planning

The next tactic is planning. One of the big challenges that Product Managers face is that sales reps will generally have far too many feature requests. Oftentimes they will come back from a customer site convinced that if we just add features a, b and c we can close the sale. Their reasons for this are sometimes valid and sometimes not.

However, if you change plans constantly based on the last few sales calls your long-term product strategy will suffer and you may end up with a product that doesn't meet anyone's needs.

The way to handle this is to have a process for feature requests so that they feel like their feedback is being taken into account and being put into the product planning process. In fact, many times if you simply capture the details and assure them it will be considered the feature request will never come up again.

Let them know how to make a feature request (ideally, set up a web form to capture the details as well as the justification for the request). Show them the process for gathering requests from sales, tech support, the team, customers and other stakeholders. Then let them know how you prioritize feature requests and that if they think something is really important to provide the justification so that it is noted as important during the process. This won't always stop reps from constantly requesting features but in many cases it will make it more manageable.

It's also critical that you get the sales reps early feedback. Don't go out and write a market requirements or product requirements document without floating some of the ideas to the reps and allies on your sales team. If you really build the relationships up-front they can be a great resource when finalizing product plans.

What you don't want to do is create an MRD or a PRD, build a product, put it in front of your sales guys and have them tell you that the product is completely wrong for their customers. You want early feedback.

And finally, involve them in your customer visits. If they understand what you're doing as a Product Manager and that you're going in, asking questions and looking for customer insights you can turn it into an excellent relationship-building opportunity with them.

The account rep I mentioned in New York that I formed the alliance with viewed it as a tremendous value-add to bring in Product Managers from Apple Corporate to talk to them about what their needs were because they felt like they were being listened to and they knew the products were going to reflect their actual comments. Getting the rep and the customer involved early was a win-win for everyone.

The caveat about planning is that you have to be extremely cautious about what you do and not expose prematurely. We've probably all had this situation happen where you talk about a possible new feature and the sales rep starts to promise it as a reality, so you need to be extremely clear and up front.

Ground Rules

The last tactic is making sure you set the ground rules. This is more for smaller companies because it's harder to control at large companies. Set the ground rules about what can and can't be talked about, what can and can't be promised to customers and get alignment with the management up front.

We had one client whom the sales reps literally would promise anything they wanted. Looking at an overall company roadmap it was clear there was no way the company could deliver everything that had been promised. But no one had set the ground rules with the reps so they did whatever they needed to in order to get the sale.

As a result, customers got angry and they lost sales, so we helped them put a process in place with management. The first rule was that the executive staff agreed that no one was allowed make a promise to customers without first coming through the company's planning committee. The second rule was that when they made a request they had to back it up with the revenue number and a confidence level that they would make the sale. This changed the game—reps began to sell what they had when they had to publicly put their reputation on the line in order to get engineering to shift resources to build their pet feature.

Worksheet: Creating a plan for working with your sales team

Rank yourself from 1 to 5 where 1 indicates you don't use the tactic at all and 5 indicates you use it all the time:

Motivation
1   2   3   4   5

WIIFM
1   2   3   4   5

Identify the Target
1   2   3   4   5

Great Leads
1   2   3   4   5

Messaging
1   2   3   4   5

Excellent Sales Tools
1   2   3   4   5

Planning
1   2   3   4   5

Ground Rules

1   2   3   4   5

List three sales reps you are going to form an alliance with.

1. _____

2. _____

3. _____

5 Getting Management on Your Side

Your ability to get management on your side and supporting you will have a direct correlation to your success and to how well your product does. You can have the greatest vision, a huge market with a dire need and a team that can execute, but if your executives aren't on board it may be a lost cause.

The good news is that there are several strategies and tactics that will help you out here. The other good news is that by employing these you will be perceived as more of a leader and have a higher probability of being promoted and moving your career forward.

Five Critical Relationships

In most cases there will be between three and five people who can make or break the plans for your product. They could be Vice Presidents or Directors of Engineering, Sales or Operations. They may be a Chief Operating Officer or Chief Executive Officer. Or it might even be an admin who can make what you need happen and get you access to executives quickly when you need a decision.

Have you identified who these people are? In a startup or very small company it is usually quite obvious. In larger corporations it may be a little more difficult. Either way, you must identify who these people are and build your relationships and rapport with them. The more they know, trust and respect you the easier it is going to be to influence them and get them to buy in to your plans.

A simple strategy is to take one of these people to lunch or coffee every week. During lunch talk about your market and your customers. Don't turn it into a formal PowerPoint presentation, but instead make sure that they become convinced that you are an expert in the technology, market and business aspects of your product lines. You want to become the de facto go-to person whom everyone trusts with respect to your area.

You also want to get subtle insights into how they view the overall business, what they think about your products versus others, what their goals and rewards for meeting them are and what you can do to help them out.

If you intentionally pursue this it will have a great impact when it comes time for critical decisions to be made. Imagine walking into a meeting where you barely know the players and there are decisions being made about which products to fund, where to spend marketing and sales resources or, even worse, who in the company to let go during tough times. Now imagine walking into that same meeting after building relationships with them, understanding their hot buttons and concerns and being viewed as a competent leader in your business. Which meeting would you rather be in?

Data, Data, Data

As a Product Manager or marketer you should constantly be reading industry publications and articles related to your products and your company. You want to be known as an expert, and one of the best ways to do this is to be on top of what is happening.

As part of this effort you also want to collect statistics and data that you can have handy. Any time you express an opinion and have some data to back it up you will be perceived as more credible and more of an authority. As a Product Manager I always tried to have five to ten data points in my memory.

For example, if you work on web-based or Software as a Service (SaaS) products do you know the current market share of all of the browsers right now? With web-based or SaaS products, critical decisions are made regarding what technologies to support and which customers will and won't be able to use your website. If you know the market share of the most popular browsers and versions you can make a strong impression when other people are simply guessing at what the right decision should be.

Short and Sweet

Be terse. If there was once piece of advice I would give a Product Manager it would be to learn to communicate powerfully with very few words. Why? Because the longer you talk or write and the more that you say the less people pay attention to you. Condense your communications. Go straight to the point. People will respect you much more, and be relieved when you are communicating rather than dreading it.

There is a simple three-step formula I learned early in my career that has benefitted me many times. I have it on my wall and use it often when I am writing an email or presentation which starts to get lengthy. It goes like this:

1. *Briefly* describe the situation—include a little background information or both points of view.
2. State selected facts—only one or two (though it will be tempting to lay out your entire argument). Do *not* state your feelings.
3. Make a clear and short request of what you want to happen (or in some cases what *must* happen). Be brief and be gone.

The temptation is to want to tell the entire story and your whole argument. In some cases this will be necessary, and you can always go there if need be. But in most cases your audience will be much more receptive if you lay it out in a concise way using the points above.

Let me illustrate with an example. When I was in charge of C++ development tools for Macintosh at Symantec I was having a difficult time getting mindshare and funding to market the product. Symantec was pretty much an anti-Macintosh company (they always believed the Mac would die an early death), and to make matters worse they had insulted the Mac community and gone from 90 percent market share to 10 percent market share in 3 years.

After a few weeks on the job I became frustrated with this (they didn't exactly tell me what the real situation was before I was hired). We had an excellent new product about to be launched that had a chance of grabbing back significant market share. So I decided to go on a campaign to get the support we needed.

My first draft of an email (to the CEO, General Manager, Marketing Manager and Vice President of Marketing) went something like this:

As you all know we have ignored the Macintosh developer tools market and made some critical strategic mistakes. During the past 3 years we have gone from 90 percent market share to 10 percent market share and have lost approximately $10 million in revenues as a result. This has hurt both our quarterly and annual financial results and has essentially been a situation where we let what could have been a very profitable cash cow turn into a near breakeven situation.

When I was hired three months ago to attempt to turn around the situation I was assured that I would have the resources, both financial and personnel-wise, to be able to turn this around and regain our revenue and profits. In talking with key people in the company this has not turned out to be the case.

We are within six weeks of launching a new version of the product that is far superior to our competitors'. We can easily take back a vast majority of market share with this product because developers are always willing to switch tools if they see an advantage in terms of pro-ductivity or in terms of the quality and efficiency of the code in their final software product.

This is a real opportunity for us to re-establish the product and to show the market that Symantec is indeed committed long-term to the Macintosh developer tools market. However, I believe there is a limited window of opportunity and that after this release we may never have a chance again....

The email went on for a few more paragraphs stating all kinds of relevant and important information that I thought would help to make my case. But the fact is that no one was going to read this email—it just didn't cut to the chase.

Here is how I could have written it:

"I am writing asking for your support on an issue that will have a sizeable positive impact on our revenues and profitability. I believe we can easily make a dramatic impact with minimal investment.

Here is the situation:

- We have gone from 90 percent to 10 percent market share in the Macintosh developer tools market in 3 years.

- Our revenues have dropped so that we no longer have a $10M cash cow to fund other projects.

- We are about to launch a *far* superior product to our competitors and have a one-time chance to regain this market share and revenue.

I need full support from each of you to make this happen, including a $100K launch budget and a dedicated marketing manager to make this happen over the next six months. I have an extensive launch plan and ROI put together and I am happy to share it with anyone who wishes to see it.

Please let me know if I have your full support."

Now if you were an executive (or anyone in your company), which email would you rather read? And which one would you be more likely to agree with?

Communicate Often and with Authority

It is critical that you communicate often with your team, extended team and key influencers. They need to receive constant reinforcement that you are in charge, that your efforts are on track (or if not that contingency plans are in place to get back on track) and reassurance that your products are going to succeed.

Send out a weekly status email after weekly team meetings to your boss and the closest members of your extended team. Make this short and sweet. That way they won't have to contact you or be concerned that things might not be going well. Once a month send out an email regarding the status of your overall business to the larger list of people. If you start to do this you will be perceived as a business leader, and your fellow Product Managers will wonder why they are being left in the dust.

In these communications (and in every word that you utter, document you write and email you send) you should practice using a tone of authority. This doesn't mean that you should be condescending or imply that other people don't know what they are doing, but it does mean that you must convey complete confidence that you are an expert in your product and market. A few well-placed words spoken with authority can eliminate hours of wasted time debating.

As a Product Manager I had a trademark phrase that became associated with me that illustrates this. Oftentimes at the end of a project you are meeting to discuss the open bugs, quality level and whether the product is ready to ship or not. At several meetings like this that I participated in we had lengthy discussions. The testing team had concerns about some bugs that caused major problems for a user, but were highly unlikely to actually occur. The user interface folks usually had some additional cleanup and minor tweaks they want to make. And the engineers were either still be trying to squeeze in their pet feature or they were so exhausted that they wanted to ship it no matter what. After issues were on the table and we started to circle back to the same arguments repeatedly I just simply said, in a tone of certainty, "Ship It." And we did.

Another example of using a tone of authority was back at Netscape in their early days. Jim Barksdale was the CEO, and as you can imagine they had many critical and highly-visible decisions to be made. They also had a lot of smart people with very strong and valid opinions. Barksdale was famous for cutting to the chase when they would have meetings regarding these decisions. Everyone would air their opinions and be heard, and then he would say, "Well, there are lots of opinions here and few facts, so we are going to go with my opinion."

Carrots and Stick

As with motivating anyone, your management team is driven by thoughts of pleasure and worries about pain. The more you know about what rewards they are seeking and what situations they are trying to avoid, the more effective you will be at influencing them.

Carrots (rewards) come in a variety of flavors. Are they working towards quarterly goals in order to receive a large bonus? Are they looking to move up and want allies to help make them look good? Is there some specific challenge they are facing that you could perhaps help them solve?

Sticks (pain and punishment) also motivate people. Is your management at risk of not making their sales numbers or staying within budget? Do they have objectives that they have to meet or else they will be fired? If you company misses the quarterly numbers will they have to lay off staff?

Try to factor these in when asking for support for your product and ideas. For example, in the short email I wrote at Symantec the first thing I started off with was an immediate attention-getter for the executive team. What executive wouldn't immediately pay attention to and want to support an initiative that could potentially blow the numbers out? It's not easy, but if you can tie in your arguments to their carrots and sticks you will increase your chances of success a thousand percent.

Worksheet: Plan for getting management on your side

List the three people who are most critical to get support from in order for your product to succeed.

1. _____

2. _____

3. _____

What is your plan for building relationships and rapport with these influencers?

_____

_____

_____

State ten pieces of data that you should know off the top of your head in order to be perceived as an expert in your market.

1. _____

2. _____

3. _____

4. _____

5. _____

6. _____

7. _____

8. _____

9. _____

10. _____

6 Leading Your Team

Now we are going to talk about leadership. There are volumes of information about how to be a leader, so I am not going to go into a lot of depth here. However, I will cover the main factors that I have seen Product Managers use effectively.

You *must* become a leader in order to succeed. This doesn't mean that you have to be perceived as the person in charge of everything, but it does mean that you need to do the right things in order to have credibility and ensure that the team trusts your decisions. There are several tactics for achieving this.

Share the Credit

Make sure you always give credit to the team. Don't take credit yourself. Make sure everyone knows that the team worked hard. Point out specific individuals. I personally like to give awards. I gave a certificate once to a project manager of mine; it said thank you for being the "Project Manager Extraordinare"—she really had done an amazing job on the project. When you do things like this you will be appreciated and viewed as a leader.

You don't need to worry about whether you'll get the credit or not. What will happen is when you acknowledge other people and you really take a leadership position, people see that over time and you get far more credit than if you were formally acknowledged for your role in what needed to happen.

In addition to credit, it's absolutely critical that everything you do in terms of speaking, in terms of writing, in terms of communication, how you carry yourself, everything you do, you want to convey that you are a leader. When a crisis comes up (and it will) don't hide—brainstorm solutions, take charge and recommend the best solution.

There is a famous story about Michael Spindler, who took over as CEO after John Sculley at Apple (I don't know if this story is true). Apparently just before one of the Apple shareholder meetings a crisis had come up and the press was all over Apple about it. Rumor has it that Spindler was found sitting under his desk hiding just before the meeting because he didn't want to talk with anyone.

I highly doubt that this rumor was true. I always thought he was a good leader and was very smart (though he inherited a virtually impossible situation when he became CEO). But the point is that you don't ever want to be known as the person who hid under the desk. Step up and have the courage to lead.

It's really simple to fall into the trap of doing things quickly and hastily, and not necessarily sounding like you're truly trying to lead the team but I would highly encourage you to think about the tone that you use, to think about how you come across because if you speak effectively and you write effectively, your perception in terms of whether you're a leader and whether people should listen to you, can be dramatically increased.

Take the Blame

When things go wrong, even horribly wrong (and they will), a leader steps up and owns the blame. Don't point fingers. Don't try to pin it on the other players. Instead acknowledge your part and let everyone know what your plan is for fixing things.

Again, don't worry that you will look bad doing this. Everyone will know that there are multiple parties involved that caused the problem. The fact that you are willing to cut your team some slack and not point fingers will buy you more goodwill than you know what to do with in the future. But you have to trust that this will be the case.

Paint the Vision

By far the most important job that you have as a Product Manager is to create a strong vision for where your products need to go to be successful. Back this up with data, excellent strategic thinking and a picture of what success will mean for the company and the team (and the rewards it will bring). No one in your company is in a better position to create and communicate this vision. After all, you are the expert on customers, competition, the overall market, the business and finances and every other aspect of your product.

Create a vision that is so strong that your team and others in your company can't help but buy in and follow you. Consider this practice for your first CEO role—when it comes down to it that is what CEOs do for an entire company rather than just for a product.

Worksheet: Creating a plan for becoming a leader

Name three people you know who you consider to be excellent leaders.

1. _____

2. _____

3. _____

Ask each one if they have any books or other resources on leadership that they might recommend to you. Make a prioritized reading list here.

1. _____

2. _____

3. _____

4. _____

5. _____

6. _____

7. _____

8. _____

9. _____

10. _____

Ask the best leader of the three to be your leadership mentor. Meet with your mentor often, get his or her ideas and create and share a plan for your own leadership development.

7 Doubling Productivity

Product Management and Product Marketing can be the most exciting jobs around, yet many people (myself included) burn out. Over the years I have sacrificed time with my family, my health and other important areas of my life because I was working very hard. The goal of this chapter is to help you work smarter, not harder, so that you can stay in Product Management for the long run and not have to sacrifice your quality of life.

Do you ever feel like there is too much work and too many priorities for you to cope with? Does it feel overwhelming and stressful at times? Are you sometimes unsure what the right next thing to work on is? Or are you looking to get that next promotion but just can't seem to break through?

Many times when I was Product Manager this is how I would feel. I was overworked. There were lots of fire drills. I was inundated with email and my To-Do list was always far too long. I had too many priorities and not enough time.

What we're going to talk about in this chapter are the productivity techniques that are going to help you so you won't feel quite so overwhelmed. The goal is to help you focus on what's important, give you tips and techniques that will free up your time, reduce your stress, and ultimately give you the rewards that you want.

Those rewards could be just the ability to go home at five o'clock every day or not have to work on the weekend because you are getting your deliverables done. Or they could be moving your career forward by working on something that's much higher visibility and freeing up your time to become a real leader in your company. Whatever your goal I think you'll find these techniques will be helpful.

How Your Boss Views You

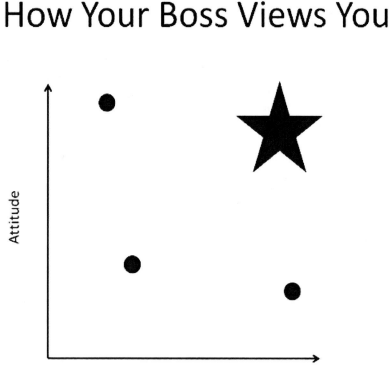

This is a chart that shows a mental map of how I viewed my employees when I was a manager. It's likely that your boss is using something similar to this whether they realize it or not. The idea here is that an employee who has a really excellent attitude and is really productive and gets great work done is the one who's going to really shine and be the real star in a company.

On the other hand, if you're overwhelmed, have far too much work and are spread too thin, one of two things is going to happen.

First, you may become too stressed out and become jaded. This happens all the time with Product Managers. They've been doing the job for a long time and haven't found the right techniques to handle things and they end up becoming cynical or negative. At that point they become branded in their company. It doesn't matter how much good work they get done, if they are viewed as having a bad attitude, it's going to hamper their success.

On the flip side, you can have the best attitude ever but you take on far too many things and be spread too thin so you are not able to get major things done. In this case you are also going to be viewed as an under-achiever.

The goal is to find a balance so that you can have a great attitude and be highly productive. So first we need to define productivity. This is something I was taught very early in my career by one of the directors I worked for when I was a young Product Manager.

In your company the majority of people don't know exactly what a Product Manager does. As a Product Manager you spend a lot of time doing tactical things because you have to do everything that is necessary to get your product to market successfully. But many of those things won't be visible or meaningful to the rest of the company.

What will be visible is major deliverables. Whether you're working on a strategic plan, a project with company-wide impact or working on critical tasks or trying to meet important deadlines that are very visible in the company, that's what you're going to be measured on and re-membered by.

I'll give you a good example of this. When I worked at Claris years and years ago, there was a woman there who was Product Manager. She did the typical Product Management tasks—running her team meetings, keeping track of details, reviewing the QA and beta plans, writing the Read Me file for her releases and so on. But she also managed to free up enough time to take on a big project for the company which entailed completely revamping all of the packaging for the company.

What happened was she did an absolutely incredible job on the packaging. And everyone in the company knew who she was and knew about that particular deliverable and that the results were her doing. If she hadn't freed up the time to be able to do something visible like that most of the people in the company would have said, "I'm not really sure what she does; she's a Product Manager, whatever that means." Instead she became known as a leader and someone who could get things done.

Your goal, if you want to move your career forward, is to think in terms of deliverables. When you get to your next review, you want to be able to say to your boss, "Here are the five things I did that had a huge impact on our company."

With that as a background, we're going to do sort of a David Letterman top ten list—top ten techniques to boost productivity. None of these are rocket science and some of them will seem very trivial. However, if you add them all up over the course of a day, a week or a year, you'll find they'll make a tremendous difference with respect to how much you can get done.

I should mention that everything I'll be covering here I've learned over the last 25 years and personally incorporated into my daily work habits. They are tried and tested techniques. Take the ones that you want and leave the ones that don't.

Technique One: Mastering Email

The first productivity-killing topic is email. Even though I can't see or hear you I imagine there's a big groan when we talk about email. I get 120–140 emails a day. If you don't have a system for email it will overwhelm you and break your spirit.

I handle email with a number of tactics. First, I make an absolute commitment to myself to not continuously process (i.e. read, respond and react) email throughout the day. Notice I said process and not "check."

I process email three times a day. I come in a few minutes early just to do this, uninterrupted, in the morning. Then I process it right after lunch and then again at the end of the day. I use a Blackberry with email access to check for urgent messages and changed or cancelled meetings and prune my messages along the way. If there's something that's absolutely critical, I'll address it but I am careful to not fall into the trap of falling into constant email fire drills. Each processing session takes approximately 15 minutes, and I try to limit my email work to less than an hour a day.

Here's the way I go about processing my email. First, I make a commitment that I'm going to get through it as quickly as I can. Then I start scouring the messages very rapidly, making split second decisions.

- If an email is spam or not even close to being relevant or important instantly I delete it.

- If it's an email where I can respond quickly I will send a very short response that usually takes less than 5 seconds. My responses tend to be just a few words like "Great we'll talk about it at the meeting," or "Approved." The idea is to not waste time on these emails.

- If it is an email that is very long that I need to read completely but is not urgent I put it in a folder called "Read Later" (I also have rules set up that automatically put newsletters, industry publications, etc. in this folder).

NOTE: For these emails I put in one to two dedicated hours on my calendar once a week for reading.

- If it's an email that's going to require a long response and a lot of thinking, I turn it into an Outlook Task so that it shows up on my To-Do list and I can prioritize it with everything else that I need to do.

NOTE: In Outlook if you right-click and drag an email to the bottom left hand corner where it says "Tasks" you can turn it into a task with the actual email attached and put it on your priority list.

If you use this method you can get through your incoming email very quickly and get onto creating an actual priority list and working from there (more on prioritizing your To-Do list later in the book).

The second tactic for email is to separate your work and your personal email. Do your personal email on your own time and use a different email address. Make your commitment that when you do your work email you are going to do it as quickly and efficiently as you possibly can. Take your personal email offline for after hours and weekends.

A third email tactic is turn off Outlook notifications (those little messages that appear reminding you that you have yet another email that has arrived). It's tempting to keep this turned on. You'll be sitting there working, a screen will pop up, it says you have new mail and you will almost instantly want to stop what you're doing and jump to it.

Nothing will slow you down more than having a constant interruption like this. Paying attention to the message is one of the worst things you can do because you really need to focus on the task at hand, so I turn notifications completely off.

The fourth email tactic is to master and use keyboard shortcuts. If you learn keyboard shortcuts really well while you're processing your email, you can fly through it. I can get through dozens of emails in 5–10 minutes. Some of my favorites in Outlook are:

- Alt S – this saves and sends your email in one step

- F9 – this sends and receives email from all accounts

- Control 1 – takes you to the email view

- Control 2 – takes you to the calendar view

- Control 3 – takes you the contacts view

- Control D – deletes the message

- Control F – forwards the message

Whether you use Outlook or another mail client invest the time to learn the keyboard shortcuts—you'll be amazed at how efficient you can be. Combine that with the email processing method I described and you'll find you can fly through email.

The other email tactic that I use is that I try to avoid jumping into long and controversial threads that go on and on for hours or days with lots of opinions. Usually what happens is people chime in; they go back and forth, back and forth, and it's very tempting to want to jump in, state your opinion, etc. But next time this happens I want you to intentionally not spend your time or energy putting your two cents in. What you will find is that if you let the threads wear themselves out, about 50 percent of them (or more) actually resolve themselves on their own without any need for your involvement.

For the other 50 percent it is to your benefit to see what everybody else is going to say first, then you can jump in and provide an intelligent response later. I can't even begin to tell you how many hours this tactic has saved me—try it for yourself.

If you can get good at these tactics and processing your email you can actually leave the office many nights and on Fridays with your inbox completely empty and everything turned into a task or to be read later. You will be amazed at just how much of a relief it is to get to this point. There's something psychological about having a massive amount of email that's sitting there waiting for you first thing in the morning. If you can clear things out and clear your head you'll find it's a big benefit.

Technique Two: Master Outlook

The second tip is to master Outlook or whatever email/calendar/contact manager software you choose to use.

I've heard lots of people complain about Outlook—they hate it, it's confusing—it's a Microsoft product. I was one of those people for a long time. Outlook has just a boatload of features, is complex and the menu system can be confusing. It is not very well understood by most users, and I frankly had difficulty with it despite the fact that I consider myself to be very good at learning new software. But at one point I decided that Outlook was the tool I was going to use and I invested in it. I went out and got the Outlook for Dummies book. I spent probably 4 or 5 hours studying the book and learning every tip and technique and shortcut. I learned about how things work under the hood and mastered many of the powerful features it has to offer. That was probably the best 4 or 5 hours that I have invested in a long time.

What ultimately happened is that after I spent those few hours I found that it literally pays off for me every single day. I save *so* much time and am able to run my life and business very efficiently as a result. I would highly encourage you, no matter what program you use for email and for organizing things, to invest some time in mastering it.

Technique Three: Work From Only One To-Do List

This next technique is to work from only one To-Do list. Once you try this you will find that it is a very different way of working. If you think about it, right now you probably have a few voicemails on your cell phone. You might also have voicemails on your business land line. You've got some emails, probably have a To-Do list, and may even have post it notes and notes from a meeting that have action items as well. So with all these competing sources, how are you going to know what's important and what you should be doing—today? How can you possibly know what is most important to accomplish by the end of today when you have all of these competing priorities scattered randomly across all these places?

What I do is that I take absolutely everything and turn it into a task in Outlook. If a client calls me and says they need something done I immediately capture it via my phone or Outlook (which synchronize wirelessly). When I get an email that is important and will take a fair amount of time I turn it into a task. And when voicemails come in instead of letting them pile up and have 5, 7 or 9 to listen to I write them down immediately, turn them into tasks and delete them from voicemail.

When you use this technique you will now have one master list of everything you need to pay attention to. You can then use this as the context to prioritize everything that's on the list against each other. This is a tremendous benefit because it relieves the stress of worrying about all of the multiple lists and lets you focus your energy and decide what is truly important.

The other benefit of doing this is as you go along your day is that when you have ideas for new projects or new tasks or creative ideas, you can instantly capture them. So you never have to worry about whether you forget about that good idea or whether you are missing something. You instantly capture everything and you have one master list that you can always work from.

Once you've got the list, what you want to do is use a proven system that works for getting it under control. The list technique that I use comes from a book named *Total Workday Control using Microsoft Outlook*. This was a book that a former client of mine recommended to me—I found it to be tremendously valuable. I highly recommend that you get a copy. I don't use everything he recommends in the book because it's a little over the top but I use a combination of that and some other things I've learned.

Another excellent system is the Franklin Planner system. The idea behind Franklin Planner is once you've got a master list, you categorize things using the ABC method. A items absolutely must get done today. B items are something I'd like to get done today if possible. C items stay on the list but are things that I don't even need to think about today.

With everything in your master list sit down for 10 minutes at the beginning of the every day and dedicate it to just planning. Rank everything A, B or C. You really only want five to ten A tasks and five to ten B tasks. If you think about it, if you got the top 20 things on your list done in any given day you would be way ahead of the game.

After you have assigned all A and B tasks give each one a number from 1 to n in terms of importance and what needs to get done. This is sometimes difficult but it forces you to make a decision about what's important. If you do this religiously you will end up with the sense of exactly what's most important and what you should be working on at any given moment.

Another really important thing about this is try not to go back an hour later and start re-visiting or re-prioritizing. Put a stake in the ground at the beginning of the day. The one caveat is that if there are critical fire drills or other really important things that show up, you may want to adjust your A items. For example, if your boss comes in and says drop everything, you may want to put that particular request on the A list.

What you'll end up with, based on this technique, is a prioritized list where you can always know what the most important things are that you must get done today and what order you should work on them. You can then start working from the top down, and make a commitment to get as many tasks done as you possibly can.

A	1	☐	Incorporate MRD Comments
A	2	☐	Summarize meeting with XYZ partner
A	3	☐	Prepare for review
A	4	☐	Comments to team on user interface
A	5	☐	Send licensing email to VP

This is the way my To-Do list looks in Outlook. At any point in time I can pull it up and with a good sense of certainty, know exactly what I should be focusing on.

Technique Four: Mastering Meetings

I am sure most of you spend a lot of wasted time in meetings every week. I never really realized how much time is wasted in corporate meetings until I became an independent consultant. You'd be amazed once you're not sitting in meetings wasting time how much work you can get done.

The first tactic I have for meetings is that whenever you can possibly do it, opt out of the meeting. If it's not absolutely critical, don't go. Don't sign up for it. Or if it's somewhat critical, go every other week. If you take a meeting that's a weekly meeting and you decide to go every other week, you've just freed up 26 hours for the next year. If you take those 26 hours and focus on deliverables or something really important for your company, imagine what it will do for your career, your next review, etc.

If you can't opt out, a really good technique is to ask the team and the attendees if you can cover your portion first. Ask them if you can go over your issues in the first 10 minutes. Instead of sitting there for an hour listening to things that probably aren't relevant, if you can go first or last (and show up late) you can free up 30–45 minutes, etc.

The second technique is something that will save you a lot of time as well. When you are in charge of a meeting, if at all possible, make it a 30-minute meeting instead of an hour-long meeting. You'll be amazed at what happens when you do this. If you make it a 30-minute meeting and you insist on it, somehow miraculously you're able to cover all the same material in 30 minutes that would have taken 60 minutes because the perception is just different.

At meetings I take notes directly into Microsoft OneNote on my laptop. That way I have an electronic searchable record of everything that was said and agreed upon and all decisions. I can also copy the action items and critical items immediately and email them to all attendees before I have even left the meeting rather than having to go back and look at my written notes and spend another 15–20 minutes trying to figure things out.

The third technique is to be adamant about taking off-topic discussions off line. Nothing will waste your time more than having people talk about something at a meeting that is only relevant to just those two people. Be tough about this. When people are off topic immediately call them on it and tell them to talk about it after the meeting.

The fourth technique is to make and enforce meeting rules. If you are running a meeting or participating in a meeting, make sure you set up the ground rules for it. For example, tell everyone there's a 5-minute grace period for being late and that the meeting is starting and decisions are being made whether or not they are there.

To enforce timeliness I like to use some fun public humiliation tactics in order to get people on board. One example was a team meeting where we had a late jar where you had to put a dollar in if you were more than 5 minutes late. Another tactic is to use a white board and call it the "Late Attendees' Wall of Shame" and make a point of putting the person's name on it when they arrive. If you make it fun and create just a little bit of incentive you'll get people there on time more often.

The last technique is for your engineering team. It is simply one word: Donuts. If you want to motivate your engineers to attend meetings, make sure you motivate them with something they are really excited about. Bringing donuts to a morning meeting will amazingly get people there on time like you wouldn't believe.

I was running a team at Adobe a couple of years ago when they were a client of mine. The engineers were typical non-morning people. They usually got in around 9:30 or 10 in the morning. I absolutely had to run the meeting at 9 o'clock because I was on a tight schedule.

To solve this I brought in the absolute best donuts I could find. I got just enough so that the engineers caught on that they had to be there on time or the donuts would run out. It worked like a charm—a Product Manager should never discount the value of sugar (or caffeine) to engineers.

Technique Five: Don't Re-Invent the Wheel

As a Product Manager there are tremendous resources available to you. If you're creating things from scratch, it just doesn't make a lot of sense.

For example, get yourself a good set of Product Management templates. The 280 Group Product Manager's Toolkit includes thirty templates covering the entire product lifecycle and the Product Management Office includes over 150 templates. Get a copy of it or work with others to create an internal set of templates for your company. Any time someone sends you a document put it in an archive folder and build up your resources.

I did this for 10–12 years. After you've done this for a while whenever you need to create a document such as a Market Requirements Document (MRD), Profit and Loss statement (P&L) or Competitive Comparison you can immediately save hours of time by leveraging previous work and templates. You don't have to re-do the formatting and you don't have to figure out what should and shouldn't be included. Instead you already have a great example in your archives.

Similarly, take advantage of the Product Management training that's out there. There are all kinds of great training companies. The 280 Group offers training and certification classes, and there are a number of other offerings. There are also excellent books, such as *Software Product Management Essentials* by Alyssa Dver and my previous book, *Expert Product Management*.

Too often I see Product Managers who are tasked with taking something on and rather than leveraging resources they create everything from scratch. A great example of this is running a beta program. There's no reason to make up your own beta program plan and figure out what should or shouldn't happen. Go get a good template or a good book that covers it.

There are many other resources that you can leverage as well. You'll find all kinds of free resources at http://www.280group.com including Product Management Associations, mailing lists, white papers, free templates and more. There are also great management blogs (my blog is Product Management 2.0 at http://www.280group.com/blog), newsletters and conferences. The more you leverage the knowledge and work that is out there, the more your boss is going to view you as highly productive.

Technique Six: Use and Master Great Tools

This technique is one of those things where the little details add up. For example, at one point I worked for a client who insisted I use one of their desktop computers. I would literally sit there and wait minutes for programs to boot before I could do any work. I probably wasted about 15–20 minutes a day just waiting for the computer.

Tell your boss you want a fast computer and a big screen so you can crank out more work. I replace my machines every 2–3 years and buy top of the line. I never sit around waiting for my computer—I don't have time to do so.

Also get a good Smartphone. This is important for a couple of reasons. You'll be able to check email during the day very quickly to see if there's something absolutely critical to respond and you can carry your prioritized To-Do list with you. And when a new task comes up just put it in your phone in your priority list so it never gets lost in the shuffle.

There are also several software products that boost productivity. SnagIt is something I think every Product Manager should own. It is a great little piece of software that lets you take screen shots and add captions and do things very quickly.

Address Grabber is also good. It takes the information from emails you receive and lets you enter it into Outlook contacts with one click. There is a new product on the market that is even better named Gwabbit. Don't waste your time manually adding people.

It is also critical that you have great search set up on your computer. In Outlook 2007 there is an instant search function built in that can save you a lot of time. I have 15,000 emails archived in Outlook and it will search the entire database in a very thorough way in about 3 seconds so I don't sit around waiting.

Correspondingly, get a good desktop search program. Vista has an excellent search built in. You can also use Google desktop. What you don't want to do is waste 10 or 15 minutes a day navigating around the folders on your hard drive trying to find what you need. You want everything indexed, and you want to be able to search very quickly.

Take a day to thoroughly learn every program that you use and all of the tips and tricks of your system. I'm betting that spending one day will result in weeks of gained productivity over the coming years.

Technique Seven: Be Politely Rude

There are all kinds of people who are going to try to waste your time every day. Sales people, headhunters, people who talk to you in the hallway and many others. You may not have any desire to talk to them but they are going to try regardless to suck up your time. Add to this unsolicited emails or requests from people you don't know (or barely know) and you can lose a lot of time in any given week.

My strategy here is respond to people very briefly and tactfully, and then move on. When a sales person calls me, I immediately tell them, "No thanks, I am not interested," and I hang up. I don't even give them a chance to pull me into a conversation. Correspondingly when a headhunter calls me about a job opening, I'm very straightforward as well. It's very tempting to talk to headhunters. They'll always tell you that the grass is greener on the other side of the fence. You can waste hours and hours talking to them (and even interviewing). But before you waste your time make a decision. Are you committed to your job or not? If not, start a job search immediately. If so, politely tell them to send the job description so that you can forward it to anybody you know.

With a little practice it becomes fairly easy to turn what used to be 5–10 minute conversations into a firm but friendly 1-minute conversation so you can get on with the important things.

Technique Eight: Stick to a Routine

Routines help us to stay disciplined and focused on what is most important. If you do the morning planning and the email processing routines they will save you a lot of wasted time later in the day. Additionally, one of the biggest time wasters is jumping onto the web and looking at story after story multiple times during the day. Spend 10 minutes right after your planning and email to check the web and then check it again at the end of the day.

In terms of planning, I do 10 minutes of planning every morning and then I do a weekly check-in to do a bigger picture check on whether am I really focusing on what's important. I also block off thinking time and reading time on my calendar and I keep the appointment. I find that if I don't put a dedicated hour or two on my calendar every week to think about strategic issues it won't happen.

You may want to tell your boss what you are doing and ask if you can take one morning a week or one day a week to work at a local coffee shop or at home to think through strategies and big projects. Getting away from the office and noise and interruptions can help you rise above the noise of daily Product Management.

Technique Nine: Get Help

If you're overwhelmed and have far too much work assigned to you, find someone to help you out. You might consider using a contractor or consultant. If you've never hired one, there's a white paper at http://www.280group.com that tells you all about it. There's a checklist of what to look for and how to figure out if the fees are right, and so on.

In addition to contractors there are many other places to get help. You might get your admin to do some of the lower level tactical work or convince your boss to bring a junior Product Manager into the group to handle the tactical tasks across multiple Product Managers.

Another excellent strategy is find someone to mentor who will help you with the work in their spare time. If you have something that you can teach and share with someone many times they will be more than willing to go above and beyond in order to help you out.

Leverage your peers and leverage the Product Management associations as well. Don't try to be a lone cowboy who's trying to come up with a unique solution to something that's already been solved thousands of times.

Technique Ten: Set Personal Deadlines

This last technique is by far the most important. It is to set strict deadlines for yourself and commit them.

Once you set a deadline you will be amazed at how things magically fall into place to allow you to get the work done. Once you write the deadline down, you have a 99 percent probability of hitting the deadline. Without deadlines, priorities shift and things fall through the cracks. So set deadlines and make these relevant to the big, high visibility things you are doing for your company. That way you'll shine and be viewed as a great employee.

Worksheet: Creating a plan for becoming more productive

List three highly-visible deliverables you are working on this quarter that will help you be known as a leader (you may need to take the initiative to create these on your own).

1. _____

2. _____

3. _____

Circle all of the techniques you are committed to trying for the next 30 days.

1. Master email
2. Master Outlook (or your email/organizer software)
3. Work from only one To-Do list
4. Master meetings
5. Don't reinvent the wheel
6. Use and master great tools
7. Be politely rude
8. Stick to a routine
9. Get help
10. Set personal deadlines

Set a deadline for a specific deliverable you are working on. Write it down and commit to hitting the date. Make the schedule aggressive but not impossible.

Deliverable: _____

Date I am committing to be finished: _____

8 Career Acceleration

This chapter is all about how to accelerate your Product Management career. Many of the techniques are things I've seen used by my peers that have worked very successfully. Some of them are ones that I have even used. Some are common sense. Some took me many years to figure out. I'm hoping that by sharing them with you, it will help you move forward towards your goals and what you'd like to achieve.

Goals

The first thing that I want you to do is spend a little bit of time thinking about your career. Sit by yourself and do some writing or jot some notes down about this. Where are you now in your career, honestly? Has your career progressed the way you would like it to? What is it that you want to achieve in the coming years? Are you where you want to be? Is your career stalled or on the fast track?

Next I want you to start to envision short term and long term goals. Think about where you want to be one, three, five and ten years from now. From there we are going to start with the 10-year goal and work our way back.

In 10 years you can accomplish a tremendous amount so don't sell yourself short. If you want to be a CEO put that down, and write a paragraph that describes what that would look like. What type of company would you be running? What responsibilities would you have? How much would you be earning? What would your day-to-day life be like?

After you have completed 10 years then work your way back. What do you have to accomplish at 5 years to make the 10-year goal? Do you need to be a vice president? Answer the same questions you did for the 10-year goal, substituting 5 years instead.

Do this until you are back to the present. Try to be as specific as you can. This will provide you with a framework to use as a plan to put together at the end of this chapter for how you are going to get there.

There was one point in my career where I realized I didn't want to continue on the path of becoming a CEO in a big corporation. My next step would have been Vice President of Product Management and then probably a CEO of a start-up or a publicly held company. I did some soul searching and decided instead to start my company, the 280 Group. It was a critical decision that I made 10 years ago. I envisioned where the company would be in 10 years, and for the most part I have achieved what I pictured. I encourage you to do the same for your career.

Stars Who Rise

It's kind of baffling as you go through your career from job to job and you see some people who advance very rapidly and others who are just stuck where they are. I'm thinking of one person in particular who I worked with that within about a 3 or 4 year time-period went from being a Product Manager to being Vice President of Marketing and Product Management for a company. Within a few years he was CEO of a small startup and has held multiple CEO positions since.

On the flip side I have seen people who literally over 10–15 years have never been able to break through. Even though they desire to become a Vice President or CEO (or they think they desire it), they'll still be at the individual Product Manager level or have moved up one notch to a product line manager.

The difference between these two types of people is not necessarily competence or how smart they are. It's also not necessarily how hard they work (though if someone's not working hard that will often be obvious and drag them down). The difference is that one has a plan and specific techniques and ways they go about managing their career and moving up while the other doesn't.

Before we go into the specific techniques I want you to go back and look at the productivity section and the graph that shows attitude versus productivity. If you aren't the star in that graph it won't matter much what else you do—you have to be viewed as a great performer with an excellent attitude in order to move forward. And you also have to be viewed as a leader (see the leadership chapter).

Get a Mentor

One of the most powerful, effective and rewarding things you can do is to get a mentor. There are very few things that can move your career forward and your job satisfaction forward faster than getting a mentor.

If you're lucky this will be your boss. In my career out of about 15 different managers I was lucky to have had two of them who were excellent mentors and who cared about my career and helped me to move forward. I moved further forward in my career working for them than under all of the other managers combined.

NOTE: If you want to be an excellent manager and gain the loyalty of your employees try mentoring them and see what happens.

If your mentor is not your boss it might be an executive in your department/division or in another one. Find someone who is successful that you respect and then ask them point blank if they will mentor you if you are committed to growing and moving forward. Be bold—don't be shy or hesitant. Successful people will be more than willing to help you but you have to have the guts to ask them and the tenacity to follow through.

One of the best moves I made in my career was to ask the CEO of a start-up to be my career coach and mentor. I was scared to death to ask him but I forced myself and he accepted on the spot. He only worked with me about 1 hour a week for a limited time but it paid off (and still helps me years later).

Your mentor can also be someone who is just more senior than you or it can even be a paid coach. You might want to pay someone to just spend an hour a week discussing where you're at, brainstorming your challenges and figuring out how to rise above it. All that matters is that the person has something that you want and you are willing to ask and work for it. So get a mentor.

Be the Bearer of Bad News

This technique isn't blatantly obvious—but you always want to be the bearer of bad news. And you want to deliver it as quickly as possible when things go wrong. What I mean by this is that you want your boss and the management to hear the bad news from you before they hear it from someone else and it becomes a huge problem for them so that they have to call you.

When something goes wrong (and it will) you want to reassure your boss and the executives as quickly as possible. Let them know what has happened and that you are on top of the situation. If you can, come up with two or three solutions and give them a recommendation for what you believe is the best way to solve the problem.

If you've ever been a manager or ever had a team that you run, the employees who do this and come to you with a solution are gold. They are the ones you want to stick up for and help with their careers. If you are part of the solution instead of part of the problem you'll be perceived as someone who takes on challenges, which will lead to op-portunities for you.

Keep Careful Company

The next concept is to keep careful company. Why? Because you are perceived to be very similar to those you hang out with. If you hang out with winners who are upwardly mobile then that is how people will think of you. And vice versa.

Early in my career I hung out with people who were pretty junior at one company I worked at. What happened was that I ended up as being branded as being pretty junior because of who I was spending time with. When opportunities came up it was difficult for people to view me as being senior enough to be able to handle the challenge and I wasn't promoted.

At the same time, there was a Product Manager who was spending time with people who were about two levels above him. He would take them out to lunch, get to know them and be seen with them at functions and events. He got promoted rapidly. He also had lifelong relationships that were very powerful. One of the people he was networking with ended up becoming a very successful entrepreneur and venture capitalist in Silicon Valley who ended up funding his startup years later.

He became branded within the company as someone who was far more senior because of who he was spending time with. This is what you want to do—find people who are dedicated to rising rapidly in their careers and rise with them. Every relationship you are building at your company right now can pay off for years. Correspondingly, if you do the wrong thing it can haunt you for years too.

Last but not least, avoid negative people at all costs. If there are jaded people at your company who are pessimistic, have bad attitudes or talk negatively you want to avoid them like the plague. If you don't you'll be branded as jaded and negative and your career will go nowhere.

Become the Expert

The next concept is to become an expert for your areas of responsibility.

You have to be the expert on your market and products. You need to have solid data and excellent information so that when the team or management is discussing your product or your market you are able to step in with timely and highly relevant information. Becoming expert will brand you as someone who is truly competent and ready to move up.

The other part of becoming an expert is you need to be an expert not only in your market and products, but also in your actual discipline. Whether you do Product Management, marketing, product marketing or even finance you need to become incredibly good at it so that everyone knows you are a master of your trade.

There many ways to build your expertise. For your market you should to set up a Google News Search and search for anything that is relevant and happening. Read and study all of the market analysis and everything you can get your hands on. Study your competitors and analyze their marketing and product strategies. And follow your company and its main competitors so that you know the big picture.

For the discipline of Product Management or product marketing you might want to attend a training course, and read books, newsletters and blogs. Or you can get involved at conferences and speak or publish your ideas to gain notoriety.

Beef Up Your Resume—Build Your Brand

The next concept is to beef up your resume and build your brand. Your resume is essentially your brochure. It is the piece of marketing collateral that will or won't get you in the door to talk to someone about a great new opportunity. You should keep it constantly updated—you never know how secure your job really is and you may need it at a moment's notice.

I would highly encourage you to find opportunities to volunteer as a way to differentiate yourself to employers. For example, I spent 3 years as the President of the Silicon Valley Product Management Association. The organization has 550 members and they are constantly looking for volunteers. Having this on your resume will help you stand out. There are Product Management associations throughout the world that need help, so why not chip in? (You'll also build a great network of local Product Management professionals by doing so).

I would also recommend that you consider taking one or more certifications. For example, I am a CPM (Certified Product Manager) and a CPMM (Certified Product Marketing Manager) through the AIPMM (Association of International Product Marketing and Management). You can also be certified in specific methodologies such as those offered by the 280 Group. All of these are ways to help you stand out as an expert and someone who has proven competence in your field.

The next recommendation is to take advantage of internal opportunities at your company to contribute and lead. I once volunteered to be on the Apple Developer Conference Planning Committee years ago. I got great visibility throughout the company, was able to contribute to a cause that I believed in and had a nice differentiator to put on my resume.

Be the Kind of Employee You Want to Manage

I don't know how many of you are managers or have managed people but there are two kinds of employees. There are problem employees and there are solution employees. You want to be a solution employee.

The way I used to make it easy for my bosses and be a solution employee is to intentionally manage them. Whether they wanted to or not, I would give them a weekly update and let them know all of the day-to-day work and the large scale deliverables that I accomplished that week. I would also tell them what I was working on next week and if there were any issues or anything I needed their input on. If there was an issue I would always come to them with solutions. I made it a no-brainer to manage me—they always knew I was on top of things.

If you're that kind of an employee your boss will absolutely love you and be on your side and willing to help you move forward when you're ready for your next advancement. In particular, if you can free up your time and volunteer to take things off your manager's plate, you'll make an even better impression.

Choose the Right Job, Boss and Company

If you are in a stagnant business segment or one that's either in maturity or decline in the product lifecycle, the opportunities are just simply going to be far less. On the other hand, if you can get into a company and market that's rapidly growing, your chances of advancing quickly are dramatically enhanced. I have seen this happen time and again—those who go where the growth is advance rapidly and those who don't get stuck.

In terms of choosing your boss, it's always hard to gauge in interviews what a person is really like. I've found from a job satisfaction and a career advancement point of view that having a really good boss who truly cares about their people and is really interested in you helping you grow your career while you do great work for them makes all the difference in terms of daily quality of life. Choose carefully and ask lots of questions to the people who report to your potential future boss.

Become an Excellent Communicator

You must learn to communicate effectively and in a way that influences and inspires others to follow your ideas. You have to be concise in terms of speaking and writing. And equally important you must master how to use tone to deliver your message in a manner that people listen. You need to learn to speak with the authority of the position that you want next.

For example, if something went wrong on your project, and you didn't feel the product was ready to ship, you might say to your team in a somewhat meek tone (knowing they are dying to be done with it), "I'm really not sure that we're ready to ship this. I'm concerned about this and this, and this problem over here."

Another way to deliver the message would to use a confident and strong tone and tell them, "Sorry, but we aren't anywhere near ready to ship this product. I have severe concerns about it that we need to address before we move forward."

Oftentimes all it takes is the right tone to end a contentious question or a debate that could take you down a real rat hole. Spoken with authority, many comments are perceived as reality.

So become an excellent communicator. If you have a local toastmaster's group, join it and practice giving presentations and getting feedback. And if you can, get a communications coach.

Hire Only Those Who Can Overtake You

When you build your team you want people reporting to you who you believe can easily do your job in a short period of time. Although this may seem counter-intuitive, I have seen it work wonders for people in terms of rocketing them to the next level.

The reason why this works is that your team *is* your brand. If you hire stars you are perceived as a star. If you hire a B player then that is your brand. Think about it this way—it is the mentors you have that will help to pull you up but it is your team that will push you up.

The other important part about hiring is that you must be committed to cultivating loyalty. If you hire excellent people and you let them know you're committed to helping them move forward, you don't have to worry about them taking your job. They'll be loyal to you and help you move up ahead of them.

Truly Care About People

Those who truly care about people and do what they can to help them always seem to get the lucky breaks. There are some exceptions to this, but for the most part the people I have worked with who are genuinely good people have reaped much success.

I can't even tell you how many favors I do for people every week. I have a network of over 5,000 people in my Outlook contacts database. Favors come back to you tenfold. Everyone who you do favors for and all of the people you work with will reappear later in your career, so that favors you do now will always pay off later.

One piece of advice I would give you is to never, ever speak badly about anyone. I'll give you a simple example. When I was working at Claris years and years ago, a new employee came on board who had transferred from another division. I thought he was the biggest jerk in the world. I thought he was arrogant. I thought he was incompetent and I almost spoke out publicly a couple of times about him. But I bit my tongue.

Interestingly, I found myself 4 years later with him as my boss, through a strange combination of circumstances. It turns out he ended up being one of my best bosses, and he helped promote me. Had I spoken out against him earlier, it's possible he would have fired me.

You are going to work with all the people you are around right now for years and years to come. Do them as many favors as you can because at some point, you may need to call on them to do you a favor and that may be the way you get your next great job.

Always Be Professional

This may seem pretty obvious, but you would be surprised at how many people overreact and come across in an unprofessional manner. Don't make issues personal. Don't make it about the person you are arguing with—make it about the issue. Get your perspective before communicating. I do this constantly. I'll write a response email and put it in my draft email folder and just sit on it and wait for a couple of hours before I send it. Inevitably when I read it again I re-write it before I send it. You don't want to be known as somebody who goes off the handle in an unprofessional manner.

Active Listening

I won't say much about it here, but if you don't know the concept of active listening you should look it up and learn about it. It is an incredibly powerful tool. It is a way to defuse situations that are emotionally overcharged and to get people who are very upset to calm down and get to a solution much faster. I was lucky to learn this technique early in my career. Learn it and use it—it will save the day many times for you.

The Last Thing You Do

Back when I was with Apple years ago, there was a Product Manager who had done just a phenomenal job. She had done excellent work for the company and had a great reputation. Then there was a re-org and she got some assignments she didn't like and she disagreed with who her new boss was going to be. The result? She walked off the job that day with no notice because she was so frustrated.

It's funny, but for some reason you are always remembered by the very last thing that you do at a company. When people talk about that same Product Manager they always remember that she walked off the job, but they rarely remember all of her great accomplishments. You'll be surprised at how many people you see that make this mistake.

When you leave a company or job you want to make it stellar. You want to leave with class. In fact, you want to go out of your way to do something particularly good because that will be the lasting impression.

Don't Stay Too Long

Don't stay too long in your job or your company. I was guilty of this early in my career, and there was a certain point where I became pretty jaded. If you can't be positive, can't have that combination of a great attitude and productivity—then you need to get a new job or new company.

If you stay too long and you become branded as being negative it can really hurt you. I've only ever seen one person who turned around the perception of being jaded, and she was able to do it successfully but it was not easy because everyone thought of her as a problem employee.

You also don't want to stay too long because there is likely to be an invisible ceiling for you. When you join a company you are perceived at the level you are currently at. Some people break through this perception, but most don't. They might get one or two levels above their current level, but in many cases the whole company will perceive them as a more junior person. If this is the case you may have to switch companies in order to break through.

Don't Sit on the Fence

Life is just too short to be in a job or a company where you aren't happy. If you are unhappy make the change sooner rather than later—you will be glad you did. I certainly was every time that I faced the fear and moved on to the next opportunity.

Correspondingly, don't sit on the fence. If you're in a job then commit to it. When headhunters call you, just say, "No thanks." The grass will always seem greener, and if you are not committed it will show in your work and attitude. Make a commitment to stay and work hard or to leave, but don't try to play both sides at once.

Build Your Safety Net

The only safety net you have is your network and your reputation. This is the only kind of job security there is these days. Even companies that were once famous for keeping employees on for life, like IBM and HP, no longer provide any kind of guarantee. People are treated as assets and they can be let go at any point in time. It may have nothing to do with your competence, performance or dedication. You can be terminated just because some vice president had a bad day or played his political cards the wrong way.

Join Product Management associations. Network with other people in other divisions and groups in your company. Take them out to lunch. Meet them for coffee. Network with other people in other companies that you're interested in. Join LinkedIn. If you're not already in LinkedIn, join some groups and participate. If you have to and you get backed into a corner and your company has layoffs, this is the way you're going to get through it and actually thrive.

Know What You Are Good At

The last concept is to know what you're good at. Make sure that you hire and recruit people to complement your skills. And do what you like. For example, I'm not a detail person. I'm a big picture person. Put me in charge of details and I'll get it all wrong. But put me in charge of the big picture, vision and strategy and I will hit it out of the park.

If I have a good detail person working with me we make a great team. Figure out what you and your team are good at and what you all like to do and split up the work that way. You'll be ten times more successful and much more satisfied.

Worksheet: Creating a plan for career acceleration

Who are you going to choose for your mentor? When are you going to ask them? Do you have a clear plan in place for what you want from them and how often you want to meet/talk?

_____

_____

_____

_____

Where do you rank on the attitude/productivity chart?

What are three things you are good at that you should continue to focus your energy on?

1. _____

2. _____

3. _____

What are three things that you are not good at where you should get some help?

1. _____

2. _____

3. _____

9 Having Fun

I believe that having fun as a Product Manager is mandatory. Let's face it, you are under tremendous stress. Your sales reps and your engineers and managers all make demands of you. Customers complain. Tech support tells you the sky is falling. And underlying all of this is the fact that you have total responsibility for your product's success and most likely no formal authority.

If you can't find a way to have fun on a daily basis you will burn out. Your team and your co-workers will get tired of being around you. You may even become one of the jaded Product Managers out there who are ruining their reputations and careers without knowing it.

Years ago when I worked at Apple I worked with a gentleman named Mark Harlan. He and I went through some difficult times together, but we always managed to have a blast. I remember him saying one time, "If you haven't done something fun at work today then you have failed." I think he was right.

When Mark resigned and left Apple (and it was no coincidence that he did the day that he first saw a beta version of Windows 95) he left a lasting impression of fun. His nickname (and his email address) had always been RedElvis (for his red hair and the obvious comic humor related to Elvis). He sent out the usual "I'm leaving" email at Apple (there were some very meaningful things sent out when people left—we were all incredibly committed to making great products). But he also attached a sound file to the email. When you clicked on it there was the famous announcer's voice at the end of a concert years ago when all of the fans were still there waiting for a fifth encore. The announcer said, "Elvis has left the building." I still laugh when I think about this.

If you ship a great product but are miserable doing so does the end justify the means? I think not. Just do one fun thing per day, that will be more than enough for you and those around you.

Bonus Exercise:

Do something outrageously fun that your co-workers will get a laugh out of. Then email me at contact@280group.com to tell me about it.

10 Conclusion

As you can tell I love Product Management and Marketing, and I hope you do too. My goal in writing this book was to help Product Managers and Marketers to be one thousand percent more successful and satisfied with their jobs and careers. I hope I have accomplished this. I also sincerely hope that you ship dozens of amazing products and that one day I will be one of your delighted customers. After all, life is just too short to ship products that suck.

I would love to hear from you if you have additional tips, comments or suggestions regarding what has worked for you in defining, launching and marketing your products, or if you have ideas for additional templates and toolkits that you would like to see us bring to market. Feel free to email me your ideas at contact@280group.com.

A The Product Management Manifesto

I am a Product Management professional.

I am dedicated to bringing great products to market. Products that delight my customers. Products that are massively profitable for my company. Products that help change the way people work and live.

In the course of managing my products there are thousands of small decisions that must be made and tasks that must be accomplished. The sum of these can add up to a phenomenal product. I choose to own the responsibility for making this happen.

I am an expert in all areas regarding my products, customers, the market, technology, competition, channels, press, analysts, trends and anything else that must be taken into account in order to win.

I have a strong vision for my products and develop winning strategies that align with my company's goals and ensure that our investments of time, money and energy are well spent.

I am committed to using the best methodologies, tools, templates and techniques available to be more efficient and effective at my job.

I have a plan for my career and I will further my professional status by attending training courses, becoming certified and reading books, blogs and newsletters to learn best practices.

I am the voice of my customers and represent them in every critical decision that is made.

I am a leader. I develop strong alliances with everyone that I need to in order to ensure the success of my product. This includes sales people, engineers, support, customers, channel and business partners, management, the Board of Directors and anyone else necessary. Some of these people will be very difficult to work with, but I will find a way to make everyone successful as a team.

I refuse to settle for mediocrity and I will be tenacious and professional in my approach to getting the best possible results.

I believe that Product Management is one of the toughest, yet most rewarding jobs in the world. Though I will face great odds and challenges I refuse to become jaded or negative.

Though I have all of the responsibility, it is highly likely I have little or no formal authority. Therefore I will do whatever it takes to persuade others to do what is right for customers and my company.

This manifesto may be downloaded at
http://www.280group.com/pmmanifesto.pdf.

B Product Management Resources

The 280 Group website is constantly updated with the latest Product Management and Product Marketing Resources including:

- Free templates, samples and white papers

- Product Management Blogs

- Product Management & Product Marketing Books

- Product Management Associations

- Product Management Software Comparison

- Product Management Job Listing Sites

- 280 LinkedIn Product Management Group

Visit http://www.280group.com and check the "Resources" section for the most up-to-date listings. Also, be sure to subscribe to our free Product Management 2.0 newsletter at http://www.280group.com/newsletters.htm and via RSS to our "Product Management 2.0" Blog located at http://www.280group.com/blog.html.

Appendix B: Product Management Resources

C Product Management/ Marketing Templates

The 280 Group also offers Product Management & Product Marketing Toolkits, which include templates, narrated training presentations and samples. The toolkits can be purchased at http://www.280group.com and cover the following topics:

- Product Roadmap Toolkit™

- Product Launch Toolkit™

- Product Manager's Toolkit™

- Beta Program Toolkit™

- Product Review Program Toolkit™

- Developer Program Toolkit™

The 280 Group also makes a number of templates available free for download on the 280 Group website in the "Resources" section under "Free PM Tools," including the following:

- MRD Outline

- Feature Prioritization Matrix

- Beta Program Bug and Feature Database Tools

- AdWords ROI calculator

- Sample Product Roadmaps

- Developer Program Roadmap

- Developer Program Cost Estimator Tool

- Evangelism Timeline

- Competitive Feature Matrix Comparison Chart

- Product Launch Plan Marketing Budget

- Press Release

- Google AdWords Tips and Strategies

About the Author

Brian Lawley is the CEO and founder of the 280 Group. During his 25 year career in Product Management and Product Marketing he has shipped more than fifty successful products. He is the former President of the Silicon Valley Product Management Association, won the 2008 AIPMM award for Excellence in Thought Leadership for Product Management and is the author of the best-selling book, *Expert Product Management*. Mr. Lawley has been featured on CNBC's World Business Review and the Silicon Valley Business Report and writes articles for a variety of publications including the *Product Management 2.0* newsletter and Blog.

Other Happy About® Books

Purchase these books at Happy About http://happyabout.info or at other online and physical bookstores.

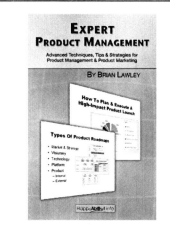

Expert Product Management

This book teaches both new and seasoned Product Managers and Product Marketers powerful and effective ways to ensure they give their products the best possible chance for success.

Paperback $19.95
eBook $14.95

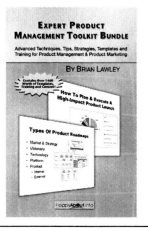

Expert Product Management Toolkit Bundle

This book includes all of the templates, knowledge, training and information that you need to make your products more successful.

Paperback $349.00
eBook $339.00

Scrappy Project Management

From the minute the project begins, all manner of changes, surprises and disasters befall them. Unfortunately most of these are PREDICTABLE and AVOIDABLE.

Paperback $19.95
eBook $14.95

42 Rules™ for Creating WE

This book offers new insights from thought leaders in neuroscience, organizational development, and brand strategy, introducing groundbreaking practices for bringing the spirit of WE to any organization, team or cause.

Paperback $19.95
eBook $14.95

CPSIA information can be obtained at www.ICGtesting.com

260771BV00003B/40/P